Circle of Soul
at the end, we begin again

By Sheila M. Burke

Om Sweet Om Publishing

Seven Hills, Ohio

Om Sweet Om Publishing

ISBN-13: 978-0615698526 (Om Sweet Om)
ISBN-10: 0615698522
Printed in the United States

Photo credit (used with permission)
Page 46 ©2012 Kelsey Burke
All other photos ©2012 Sheila M. Burke

Cover Design by Sheila M. Burke ©2012
Library of Congress Card Number – Pending
Circle of Soul: at the end, we begin again / Sheila M. Burke/ ISBN-10: 0615698522 1st Edition

Also by Sheila M. Burke:

Zen-Sational Living: A Simple Guide To Finding Your True Self and Maintaining Balance

Booyah Spirit: 52 Ingredients For A Healthy Soul. Suffering Is Optional

www.ZenSationalLiving.com

Dedication

This book is dedicated to the 17 year old me.

With Special Thanks To:

Doe Zantamata, inspirational author (and friend): for all your help with getting me to step outside of my comfort zone and publish my first poster book. *You amaze me.*

My boyz: Peter Ford, inspirational author, and Dhani: Without them this book would still be untitled. We inspire the world with our words regardless of medium. *I am grateful* for your inspiration.

The Clams: I am better for knowing all of you.

My second set of eyes and good pal, Robin Renner. (*Zebra!*)

And finally, Kiran Shaikh. Your friendship is priceless. *You inspire me.*

Introduction

You can read a lot on the matter of self discovery and you should absorb as much as you can. All of my books are written as if I'm speaking to you. I want my readers to take in my words with ease. I also know from experience how foreign the beginning of a personal journey can feel, therefore, my intent is to aid the reader in understanding everything in simple fashion. It is not hard to journey, you only need a couple of things to get on your way: an open mind, the will to move forward, and persistence. You will not play a concerto the first time you sit at the piano. Instead, you learn to play over time.

There comes a point in all our lives when we question why we are here. There is an awakening inside. It's the moment when your heart opens and longs for its Spirit, and aches for answers. It's like being lost, alone in a dense forest, with sounds of wild creatures around. Creatures you cannot see, but can be heard. All of a sudden you hear a familiar voice calling out your name. The Circle of Soul is the excitement of leaving the forest and going home to spirit. It is about looking for something bigger, a higher purpose, or a deeper meaning. It is a journey we repeat over and over to strengthen our soul. Sometimes we are younger when we start seeking answers; sometimes it is later in life. Regardless of gender we all soul search. We might reach this point in our lives through tragedy, heartache, emptiness, loss, despair, confusion, or simply through natural curiosity. Sometimes we might feel as if something is missing, *a fundamental part of our self*, that might get us on the path. It really does not matter *how* it is that you came to start your journey – the point is you *have* started. Our soul, our spirit, lives on. It is forever perfecting itself. It is a perfect circle; at the end, we begin again.

Since the beginning of time, sages, spiritual leaders, gurus, and prophets have provided us with the answers to live a spiritual life. Finding your inner spirit has never been a secret, but it helps to understand why it is that you are at this point, and why you've come so far from your inner self. This book will explain this simply and guide you to fix it.

None of my books require, ask, or suggest leaving your religion, but they are intended to strengthen your faith. Faith in God (by whatever name you call Him), faith in mankind, faith in love, and faith in *yourself*. You will not find a set of rules – merely a guide to help you find your own way.

There is no reason whatsoever to feel miserable. You might think this person or that person causes you heartache or misery, but this is simply not true. The only person who can control your happiness is you and you alone.

Understanding

The story always begins the same.

Before you took your first breath you required nothing but love, nourishment, and compassion. You awaited your birth with wonder and anticipation for your journey. Everything would be new, exciting, and fresh; you were pure Spirit. Little by little, those who care for you will taint your path. The beautiful Spirit will begin to receive layer upon layer on its Being - layers of perception, impression, and thought. These layers, over time, will become a part of you. Your Spirit, now with a human body, also inherits human tendencies.

Cliff Dwellings at Montezuma Well, AZ

In spirit form you make no distinction between souls; in human form humanity will be divided into groups and classes, colors and religions, and you will be taught that there are people that will be okay to socialize with and those who will not be. Helping others will become a game of pick and choose as labels are placed on everyone to let you know what is acceptable and what is not. Some rightly so for your safety, but more often then not this is due to your caretakers (and all their layers) imposing their beliefs and way of life upon you. *Again*, this is only human.

Montezuma Well, AZ

Children, as well as adults, flourish in an atmosphere which is nurturing; where accountability and mistakes are forgiven; where differences are celebrated and communication is always encouraged; where there is room for rules but not rigidity. Children mimic those who are around them – for good and bad. As a child grows older it is his or her strength as an individual, and strength of developed character which enables the child to filter the good from the bad – and to decide whether or not to act upon it.

Grand Canyon, USA

Children inadvertently inherit the layers of those who raise them. I'm sure no parent wants to raise a mental mess, but unfortunately many do. Unknowingly, parents can transfix their own fears and thoughts of the world, love and life upon their children.

You cannot blame them because all of us are on our own path of evolving our consciousness. If the parent is not equipped with the tools needed on their journey (or has not started their own journey) you cannot expect them to raise a spiritually strong child. Unfortunately, during the critical ages when children absorb everything - and their character begins to establish - they are learning the negatives that their caregivers are dealing with.

Sedona, AZ

So, as soon as you were born the changing of you commenced. Those around you influenced everything around you from what you ate, your choices in music, the things that made you laugh, your fears, your hopes, and everything that made you, *you*. The perceptions of how those close to you saw the world influenced your perceptions. As time went by you would develop a personality to fit these perceptions.

Over the years you remain in the rut carved out for you - getting deeper and deeper, layer upon layer, suffocating the Spirit within. You grow so outside yourself that you begin to see yourself as an outsider. As you age, the layers are also built upon by friends, teachers, co-workers, clergy, and everyone in your life. This continues throughout your life with relationships: layer upon layer is strengthened, added to, and reinforced.

Custer, SD

So begins the journey - the process of rediscovering yourself, the discarding of years and years worth of stale, moldy layers of what others painted upon your Being. Your Spirit becomes stronger as it cries out to find itself.

To pull yourself up and out of that rut you must understand that you are your own person. You must put a stop to those growing layers and begin to peel off the old ones. You will need to unravel these layers and understand why you are the way you are, and understand that everything up until now can be corrected, but you have to be willing to do a few things no matter how hard they seem right now.

All the baggage people bring into your life becomes lessons. Unfortunately, we are only as good as our teachers in deciphering them. If your caregivers were a mess, you'll have a skewed view in what you take away from these lessons. Again, you cannot blame any of them because they are doing the best they can with what tools they have at their level of consciousness. In order to heal yourself you must accept this. Everyone is at a different point in their own evolution of consciousness. This can be seen in words, thought, action, and reaction. Some can't accept anything: credit, comments, criticism, or change. Their layers are so thick that penetration of any truth other than what they believe to be true is impossible. This is not a flaw in their character, but rather the point they are at in their own Circle of Soul.

One thing to realize and accept early on in the process of your own journey is that it is not within your power to change anyone other than yourself. You must be able to understand beforehand that you have two choices: accept this behavior and adapt yourself to it, or don't accept it and move on. As you can see there is not an option for changing the other person – you either change yourself, or you move on.

Ask yourself what it is you are willing to compromise when making your decisions. Are you strengthening your character for the better by changing yourself, or are you compromising your character by changing what you believe at your core? If you do elect compromising your own internal beliefs, you should be ready to revisit the issue down the road.

Custer, SD

To understand ourselves we must look honestly at our own character, our traits, our fears, our beliefs, our support system, and our needs. The goal is to keep the positive and dump the negative. Understand that the life you are living is not how you started out, but instead has become an arm of someone else's life that imposed a layer upon you.

Now that we have talked a bit about understanding why we are the way we are due to the layers upon layers we have accumulated in life, what is it that we are supposed to do with this knowledge? This is where forgiveness and gratitude come in.

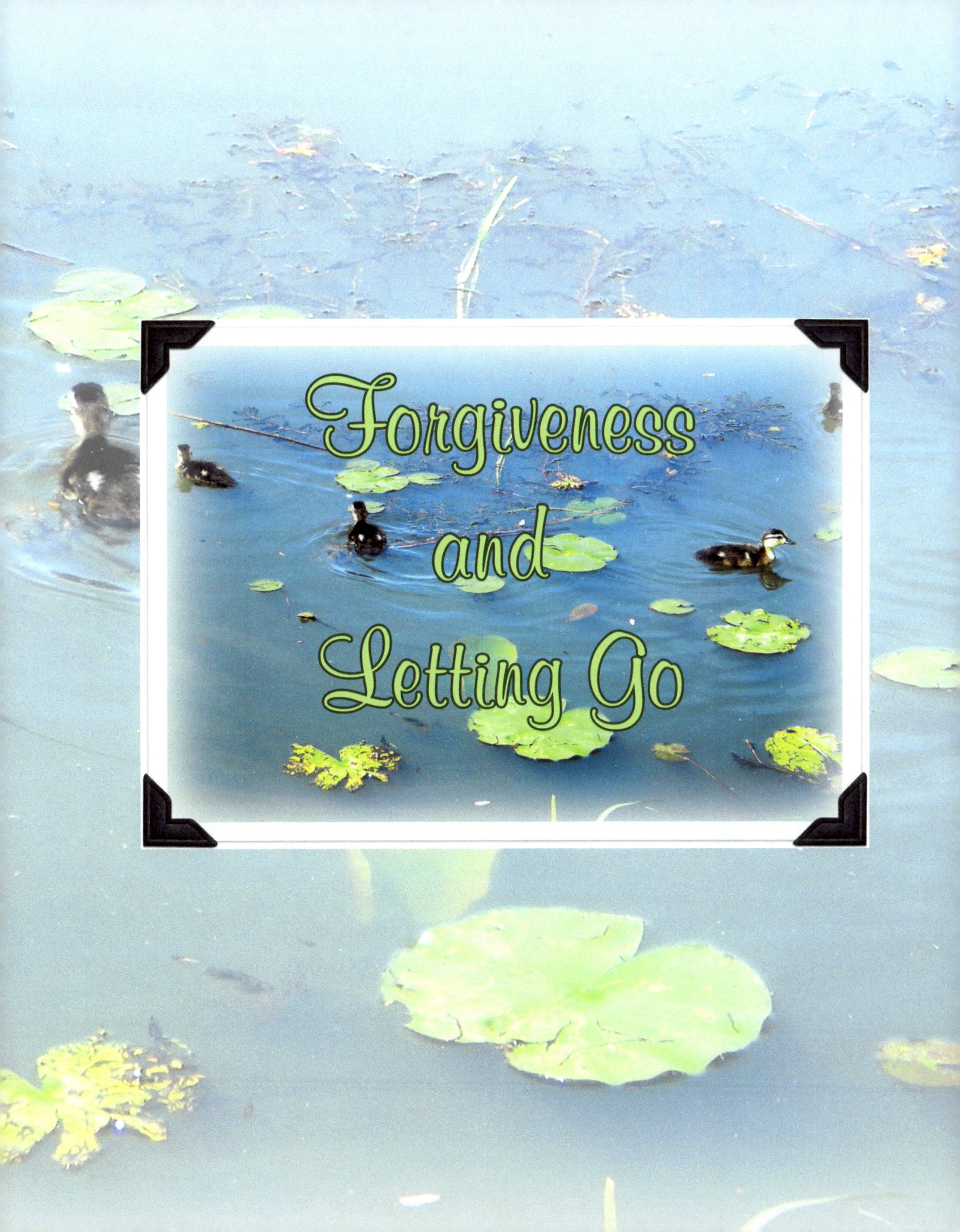
Forgiveness
and
Letting Go

Forgiveness does not mean letting people who have harmed you off the hook, or that you condone their behavior. It is a step in moving forward in your own journey. Forgiveness in this sense doesn't mean you ask for, demand, nor require an apology — it is about putting an end to your suffering through understanding that everyone is experiencing their own level of consciousness. People are going to make mistakes, they are going to say things which are hurtful and do things which are stupid sometimes. Just like you are learning, they are learning as well.

Whether or not you decide to release this person from your life altogether or not depends on the circumstance. Obviously if you are being physically or mentally harmed by them this is a good course, but more often then not there will be people you don't want to release such as a child or a parent. You might want to retain the relationship, but need to make adjustments in the health of those bonds. It is not fair to your spirit to remain stuck between loving someone and hating the dynamics between the two of you.

Forgiveness is about letting go of the anger and resentments you hold against another, as well as against yourself. Bring forth these layers of negativity, acknowledge them, and let them go. You no longer need these layers, as they have no place in the stronger, new you. There are a couple simple ways to aid in the disposing of these layers: meditation and ritual (such as writing a letter to the person expressing your feelings - and burning it). *Let's explore ritual.*

We find rituals in every culture and facet of society. We perform them for luck, cleansing, holidays, religions, and many reasons. A ritual is a little ceremony that is symbolic. It is an aid to guide your thoughts through the use of a visual aid. For instance, a great way to forgive someone is through the use of a ritual burning. *Not the person, but the pain.* The idea is to have a ceremony to heal your Spirit and to move on from the pain you are stuck in.

Combining your intent with a physical act aids in the healing process. It then becomes something tangible. The act of letting go is no longer merely from your mind, but it is a physical release.

First, you are going to write a letter to this person. It is not a letter you will ever send. Remember, you cannot change anyone, so there is no point in sending it. This is about healing yourself – not healing them. Don't hold back your feelings. Feel free to be as mean as you want to in this letter. Bring every single emotion which you are feeling into words. Go ahead and swear if you want, scream if you need to, and throw the words *nice* and *diplomatic* out of the window. Don't worry – the Universe, God, a Higher Power – Spirit; you must get it out of your system. is fully equipped to handle everything you can release, and will help you to heal your

Explain to the person what it is that they did or said that caused you such pain. State how it made you feel and how it actually affected your life. Put the letter into a safe place.

Now, in this healing ritual, it is important to get your mind into a calm and clear state for the actual release.

A great place to start is through the use of meditation. Some may use candles, burn incense, or say a prayer. Since this is a ceremony of spirit, it is essential to bring your mind, body, and spirit into a calm and relaxed state.

The next step is placing your letter with all of your emotions stated within the pages, into a container safe for burning. It is best to burn this outside rather than indoors for obvious issues, but this is also a direct path of release into the atmosphere. Now it is time to let this all go. In your ceremony you will recite something to affirm to yourself and God, the universe, a higher power, that you are ready to heal. You might say something such as, "I release all negative feelings. I replace destructive behaviors with love and respect of my self", or "I am strong, secure with my self, and I release my pain".

Whatever phrase or words you decide to use should be positive affirmations and focused on healing. Your statements should reflect what you want as if it's happening right now. For instance you are not going to say "I will release", or "I intend to release", or "I want to release", because these are all worded as future thoughts rather than focusing on the present. More positive statements would be "I am releasing", "I now release", or simply "I release".

The final part of your ceremony is to reinforce what you have set in motion. It is now time to fill the empty space where these negative feelings used to reside, with positive thoughts and energy. Figure out what you are now striving for and set your course to get there. If you were once held back, you will strive for independence; if you had been abused, you are striving for building healthy relationships and strength of self.

Continue to meditate or pray on a daily basis to help reinforce what you aim to be. It is going to take time. You might feel a loss over the destructive feelings that caused you so much grief. That is normal because you have made it a part of you, for so long. Now that you have emptied yourself of it, you now have room to fill that void with loving, healthy behavior and positive energy.

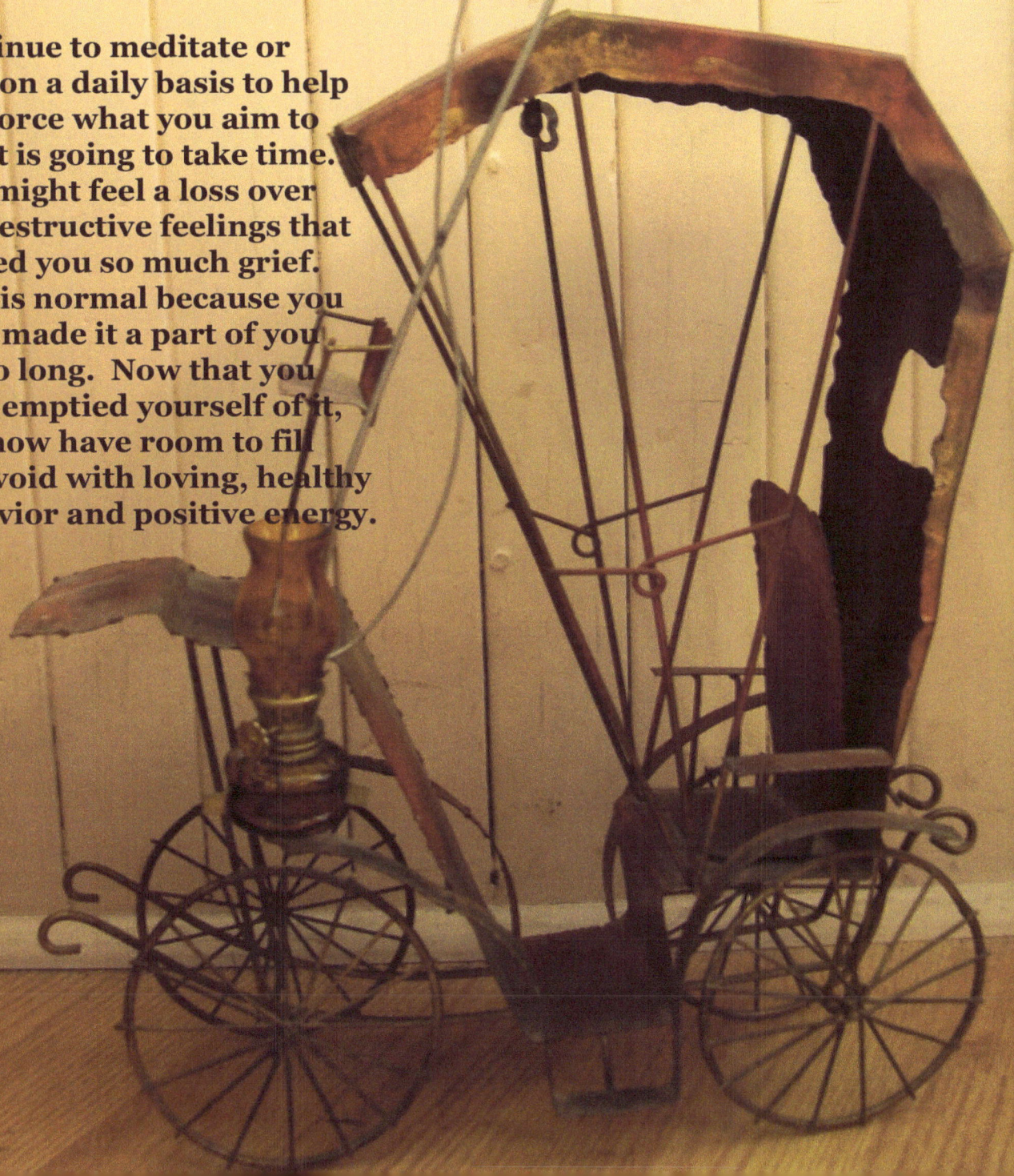

When you stop blaming others for your own issues, for what you do or don't possess, you become responsible for your own self. You begin to realize you do not need to depend on anyone else to get you where you are going – you hold all you need inside of you.

It is what you came here with and what you've cast aside over the years when your ego took over. It is your Spirit. Cast the ego, outside influences, and all the negative thinking aside and rediscover your core, your Spirit, and what It needs: love and compassion.

Finding one's self does not mean letting go of your job, your life, or everyone around you. It means strengthening your Spirit, your soul so you can be strong enough to deal with all these things. Let go of that which does not strengthen you.

Meditation is a gift to your Spirit, a gift of calm, a gift of serenity, and a gift of love. You came here as a being of love and light, and through meditation you will reconnect with self, with love, with Spirit, and with light.

Moving On

Changing your life, turning over a new leaf, or sticking to your goal of releasing your pain and focusing on the positive is really very simple. It requires only one thing: *Thinking a different thought.*

Anyone can do it at any time. Some might be reading this and think I'm crazy, or that this is impossible. Not only is this completely possible, but it works extremely well.

Bottling up your feelings, dwelling on them, or being afraid of them is very harmful to not only your mental health, but your physical health as well. With practice you can stop doing this! People may say "easier said than done", and this might be true if you are not willing to be persistent and stick to your goal of letting go of unhealthy feelings. But you are strong and you can let go of these negative thoughts and feelings! It is not a secret – you have the ability built right in to you! Allow yourself to experience the emotion, and then tell yourself you are finished thinking of it. Now, turn your attention to something else – something positive.

There is no reason to allow yourself to be bothered by something someone did or said all day long, when the act is over and done with. You experience what happened and then you have two choices: choose to let it fester, or choose to move on to something more positive.

Be aware of your breath at all times. When feeling stressed concentrate on breathing. Breathe deep through your nose slowly; quietly imagine you are breathing in calm. Feel your belly rise. Breathe out the stress slowly on the exhale.

Just the same as you have the ability to pull up a thought of something that is negative, you also have the ability at any time to pull up a thought that is positive. You can turn your attention to negative *or* positive at any time. Try this little experiment and see how easy it is: think about something sad (your pet passing away). You actually feel sad, you can feel the tension in your body, and you might feel a lump in your throat or tears welling in your eyes. Now, think of something positive (something that makes you happy).

Feel the change in your body? The tension lifts and you feel lighter; a smile forms on your face; you might even feel a bit of adrenaline. When you are feeling any negative feeling or you are thinking any negative thought, it is very important to turn that process around and think about something positive. Just as the ritual ceremony provided a visual experience to the mental thought, a visual aid will also help you with thinking another thought.

On a few note cards, write your happy thought trigger and keep the paper in your pocket, on a car visor, on the refrigerator, or near your desk.

When you feel that negative entering your mind – turn your attention to your positive trigger and blast that bad energy out of your mind.

Gratitude

An important part of healing is having gratitude for what you have, what you've had, and what you will receive. Appreciate all that is, for everything is something that enables you to learn.

There are so many gifts extended to us daily which are often taken for granted. How often do we neglect to see the value in the simple things in life: a smile from a friend, a sunrise, a storm cloud, a field of corn, or an apple tree? Learn how to fully appreciate these every day gifts which generally are not given much thought.

Wooster, OH

Listen for gifts: a streetcar going down the track, a bird chirping a familiar melody, the whistle of a policeman, or the cool breeze on a warm summer day. Every human sense is capable of reaching for those gifts whether it is the sweet aroma in a field of flowers or the rough touch of the bark on a tree.

When you are grateful and can find the love in the every day moments of life, you are tapping into a deeper awareness of all that is. When you find love you will live and express yourself as love. You will attract more love, and life will get better for the fact that you are expressing yourself through your Spirit and not through your ego.

San Francisco, CA

Take a moment, relax, and appreciate all that you experience. When your heart is filled with love, joy, and gratitude your Spirit is experiencing what it is supposed to.

San Francisco, CA

Each of us must to learn to enjoy life and live it with appreciation – not with worry or regret. We need to take responsibility for our actions, and understand that by taking away all physical features, flaws, *and awes* that we are all literally souls on the same path to the Divine. If you spend all of your earthly mission being miserable and fail to learn from life, you might be back here to try again.

Wooster, OH

In order to be truly grateful for things we must change the way we look at life, and experience it like you are seeing it for the first time – with love and joy. Parents might understand this better by recalling the birth of a child. You study the child as it sleeps, amazed by the very breath, life, and the mere fact that the child is here. Everything is new and exciting, teaming with life force. You can *feel* the light. Many people might understand this in the experience of a new love – that *takes my breath away feeling*, or that *I smile every time I see you kind of love*. It is when the thought of your love and life is fresh and exciting and every next thought leaves you giddy and alive.

All of life should be lived with the deep admiration, compassion, and love – with a feeling of euphoria and bliss. Even in difficult circumstances, for it is helping your soul attain the Divine landing it is working toward. Of course some things are sad, disturbing, and horrible, but in time you will learn to discern information from these things and let them go.

Although the human mind finds it extremely difficult to forgive – it is essential to the Spirit that it learns how.

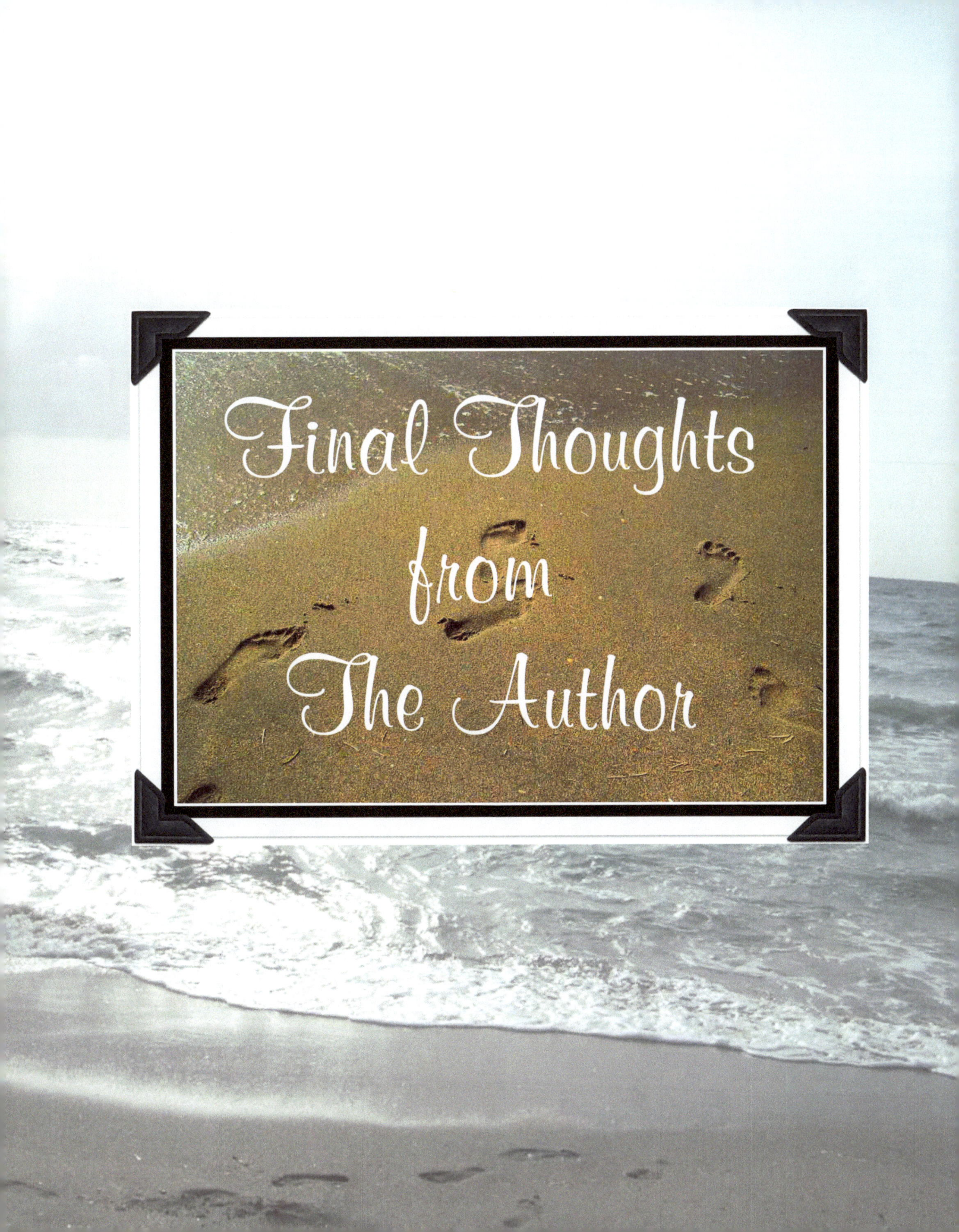
Final Thoughts
from
The Author

Sometimes I think Earth is just a place where souls come to learn. It's like a boot camp, except you spend your whole earthly life doing it. We are souls learning how to be Divine. We are in basic training, enmeshed with family units, and given obstacle courses – all with one goal – loving one another. Why is it so hard to cast aside all the garbage layers and get back to basics? I believe it is the human experience and the course of learning. If we didn't have something to fight through, we would not have a conducive learning experience.

Huntng Valley, OH

Our mission here is to love and be loved. To fight back down to our core and despite anything the universe throws at us — all the obstacles, circumstances and people — the goal is to remain in love, *not in layers*. Life will throw rocks at you; there will be days — heck, years — of hard knocks. The point is throughout it all to remain in a state of love and fight through it. When you are able to see everyone for what they are in their core, to look past the things that are annoying, difficult, and different — you will see *at the core* is the same light and love that is also in your core.

Hunting Valley, OH

We are presented with circumstances, opportunities, and obstacles to achieve that divine goal and as humans we fail at many turns, and we are too busy worrying about what our ego wants or says. How many times do you not do what you know is right - because your ego says otherwise? Your goal isn't to finish life with a lot of money or things, it is not even to simply finish. We are here to learn something – to be a loving soul; a loving Spirit. We are here to understand we are all one. We are all the same light.

Everything you do in life is an opportunity to learn this.

Cleveland, OH

We have choices to make all the time. Whether they are big or small, they are a part of your soul's journey. For instance, you can get mad at the traffic jam or the driver ahead of you or have compassion and understanding that the problem is not about you. It is not all about you being in a hurry, it's how you deal with the circumstance. Getting upset isn't going to make you get to where you are going any quicker, it is only going to make you more upset. Little things like this happen all the time, these little tests of the Spirit. No matter what it is: traffic, children, neighbors, or any small circumstance – pay attention to your reactions. Take a moment to breathe and relax before reacting.

San Francisco

The same applies for the bigger obstacles in life. It is important to come from a place of love and compassion before taking action; to come from a place of spirit rather than the ego when dealing with everything. Discover the love and light and share it. You will find it in the difference between doing something and doing nothing, between lending a hand and walking by, between a smile and a dirty look.

Hunting Valley, OH

No one is better than you; you are
no better than another. That is how
it starts out; that is how it ends. All
stuff in the middle, which we call life,
should also be the same.

Understanding this, and living this,
is what we need to accomplish in
our time here.